GOING DOWN GRAND
Poems from the Canyon

Edited by Peter Anderson and Rick Kempa

Layout and design: Harvey-Rosen

Cover art: William Henry Holmes, drawn for E.C. Dutton's 1882 report, Tertiary History of the Grand Cañon District. (U.S.G.S.)

Photographs on pages 1, 59, 111 and 148 courtesy of Brendan Swihart
Photograph on page 21 courtesy of Tomas Castelazo
Photograph on page 79 courtesy of Rick Kempa

The inside back cover is a detailed section from a U.S.G.S. geological map of the Grand Canyon.

Our thanks go out to Betty Upchurch, past curator of Grand Canyon Research Library, to Richard D. Quartaroli, formerly on the library staff at NAU, and to reference librarians at University of Utah, Northern Arizona University, Western Wyoming Community College and Adams State University, who searched far and wide to locate canyon poems. Thanks also to WWCC student interns Tay Audevart and Hannah Winward for their active and creative input. Thanks finally to the many writers who shared their poetry with us.

ISBN 978-0-9883846-5-1
First printing, July 2015

LITHIC PRESS
fine books for an old planet

www.lithicpress.com

Table of Contents

IV. Emergence

GOING DOWN GRAND
Poems from the Canyon

Introduction

The Grand Canyon is, as poet Amil Quayle suggests, a place that defies description. "Language falters and dies before the fact…" he writes. It "is its own language / Written across space, causality and time." None who try to write about the canyon are immune to spells of muteness before its vast fact. Nearly four hundred pages into his 1872 book, *The Exploration of the Colorado River and Its Canyons*, John Wesley Powell admits that "[t]he wonders of the Grand Canyon cannot be adequately represented in symbols of speech, nor by speech itself." Early 20th Century poet Henry Van Dyke, whose poem "The Grand Canyon" was immensely popular in its era, nonetheless asserts, "The great chasm…cannot be ploughed or plotted or poeticized or painted. It is too big for one to do more than creep along the rim and wonder over it." And yet, while it is true that even the best-chosen words are flimsy substitutes for being there, the poets whose work is gathered in this collection have each found ways to make their encounter with the Grand Canyon real and memorable.

"Each man sees himself in the Grand Canyon," Carl Sandburg declares in "Many Hats." "Each one brings and carries away his own Canyon." Thus, poet Joan Baranow, arriving at the brink, sees a "terrible incision, terribly gorgeous," through which a hidden river is "rubbing against rock, pursuing its prehistoric task." Parker J. Palmer's eye, by contrast, is for the "breathless emptiness," and Diana Hume George, color-struck, sees "a place so deep and bright." Some find their safe-space in the canyon: Ann Weiler Walka, cocooned in her sleeping bag in its depths, declares there to be "no other home." Others, like the cowboy in Omar Barker's poem, wishes he could tie himself "to the doggoned tree" and let his "horse go take the look." Mary Beath, in the lee of a piñon pine "trembling at the edge," peers into a "distance far too deep."

The Grand Canyon, as much as any place, invites us to consider the meaning of our endeavors and our evolving relationship with this planet. More than most places, it encourages a healthy consideration of our insignificance. "We are this small. This brief," Wendy Mnookin declares, in a poem that relies as much on space as on the few words that inhabit it. Fred Dings challenges a casual comment that he overhears on the rim—"I wish we could live here"—to consider the tenuous hold of any life form in the realm of the canyon. That particular observer, he points out, does not notice "the clutch of desert plants / struggling at his feet, which will soon die / and blow across the stones, stain the rocks, / or lodge as molecules of dust in someone's eye. / How much grandeur does it take until / our eyes fall to the small life before us, / the geologic blink we call our lives…"

The poets in this book try to articulate the wonder or the uneasiness that overcomes them as they stand on the edge of the abyss. They try to communicate what it is they feel as they thread their way across the face of deep time as revealed in the canyon's geological layers. They try to record the exhilaration of running Lava Falls or Crystal Rapids down on the Colorado River.

The tools they bring to this enterprise are not, of course, theirs alone. Explorers, scientists, and park rangers all call on devices like metaphor to evoke the experience of the canyon. In 1776, Father Garces compared it to a "calaboose," while in 1857, Lieutenant Joseph Christmas Ives saw it as "the gate of hell." Geologist Clarence Dutton, in *Tertiary History of the Grand Canyon District*, his 1882 report of seven summers spent on the North Rim, resorts to the precise language of architecture to impose order on the "confusion of multitude" that he observed from Point Sublime: "Hundreds of these mighty structures…rear their majestic heads out of the abyss, displaying their richly-molded plinths and friezes, thrusting out their gables, wing-walls, buttresses, and pilasters, and recessed with alcoves and panels." Contemporary visitors to the South Rim may glean a sense of the canyon's fathomless age on the "walking metaphor" of the Trail of Time, where each bronze marker underfoot—and there are 1,840 of them—signifies a million years. Good interpretive expression provides memorable images that help us comprehend our geographies and the reference point from which we perceive them. Sometimes metaphor works best.

But there is no substitute, in poetry as in the sciences, for writing that accurately depicts what the fine-honed senses have observed. A century and a half of study by naturalists has yielded a body of literature that excels in this regard. Few can rival Dutton's ability to evoke the big picture, as when he conjures the drama of sunset at Point Sublime: "The haze has relaxed its steely glare and has changed to a veil of transparent hue. Slowly the myriads of detail have come out and the walls are flecked with lines of minute tracery, forming a diaper of light and shade." The notebooks of generations of rangers, meanwhile, provide the close-up in the foreground: the dragonflies at Indian Garden observed by Clyde Searle in 1931, with their "four long , silver-gauze wings…beautifully veined, and…often spotted with white or amber or ruby-throated patches;" the "bluebellied lizard" lovingly described by Edwin McKee in 1928; the female Abert Squirrel that Glen E.Sturdevant watched in 1934, who carried "a mouthful of strips of juniper bark and dry pine needles" to her nest and "padded them in place."

Poets too are intimately concerned with conjuring the particulars of the world. Janet Eigner, climbing the North Kaibab Trail in spring, recites the litany of the wildflowers: "crimson Penstemon bugling ... / ... Indian Paintbrush's scarlet chimes." Thea Gavin, poised on the North Rim, observes a spider web "twist/ a bit and float/and fall upon/ the breath of red layers." And because poets, like scientists, subsist on names, Danny Rosen, chanting his way downtrail, is fueled by syllables: "down under thunder-named: / Kaibab, Toroweap, Coconino / Sandstone. Switching back / to shale… /…down karst, down travertine. / Sipping Muav seep."

Where the poet may seem to part ways with many naturalists is in trying to articulate the emotions that arise from a canyon encounter. For those lucky enough to dwell at length with the Grand Canyon, there is no keeping emotion out of the mix. Sometimes it seeps into the so-called objective accounts, as when Powell addresses "the glories and the beauties":

> [H]ere the colors of the heavens are rivaled by the colors of the rocks. The rainbow is not more replete with hues. But form and color do not exhaust all the divine qualities of the Grand Canyon. It is the land of music. The river thunders in perpetual roar, swelling in floods of music when the storm gods play upon the rocks and fading away in soft and low murmurs when the infinite blue of heaven is unveiled.

In certain moments, even scientists can be slain by beauty. Here's Dutton, transported outside himself, in a passage that proves the common ground of poets and geologists, those gazers into distances:

> All things seem to grow in beauty, power, and dimensions. What was grand before has become majestic, the majestic becomes sublime, and, ever expanding and developing, the sublime passes beyond the reach of our faculties and becomes transcendent.

"Human stories roll across the landscape" too, Mary Beath reminds us, "demanding attention, voicing / their energy," and these

Grand Canyon poets channel them. Hopi storyteller Albert Yava shares the tale of the emergence into the Fourth World from the *sipapuni* at the canyon bottom. Laura Tohe recounts her Navajo mother's bus ride, decades ago, to assume a job as a maid at El Tovar hotel. Andrea Ross and Becca Lawton offer new versions of the lives of Bessie Hyde and Georgie White that are legend to all veteran river-runners. Judith McDaniel tells of her encounter with a "child shivering in a wet t-shirt" on the Hermit Trail in a sleet storm and Yevgeny Yevtushenko of a blind girl led by "a dog on a safety leash /.../ along the edge of the abyss." We are drawn to these stories because they give us a place to stand in the midst of so much that remains inexpressible.

Humorist Irwin Cobb, in an essay that appeared in the *Saturday Evening Post* in 1913, gives the best assessment of the disclaimer about the limits of language that so many writers profess:

> Nearly everybody, on taking a first look at the Grand
> Canyon, comes right out and admits its wonders are
> absolutely indescribable—and then proceeds to write
> anywhere from two thousand to fifty thousand
> words, giving the full details. Speaking personally,
> I wish to say that I do not know anybody who has
> yet succeeded in getting away with the job.

Cobb's comment highlights a final virtue of the poets in this anthology—they aim to tell us more by saying less. Consider Bernice Lewis' summation of what makes a good canyon hike: "Last one out wins." Or Thea Gavin's injunction of what she hopes the canyon will give back to those who really see it: "burn their muscles, / scar their skin / and memory."

In his 1937 essay, "Midnight on the Desert" J.B. Priestley suggested that the Grand Canyon experience be the basis upon which to judge many human endeavors: "Is this good enough to exist in the same country as the Canyon? How would I feel about this man, this kind of art,...if I were near that Rim?" In examining the many hundreds of Grand Canyon poems that were sent to us or that we found, we asked of each a similar question: How would it read on the rim, on the river, or somewhere in between? Or, to say it slightly differently, how would this poem strike the ears, minds, and sensibilities of contemporary readers encountering the canyon?

This criterion guided us as we explored the body of canyon literature written over the last 130 years. While we have included the words of earlier poets like William Bass, Maynard Dixon, and

S. Omar Barker, many poems, notable expressions in their own era, spoke less compellingly to our modern ears. Henry Van Dyke's 1913 poem is a good example. The Victorian diction he uses to address the canyon—"What makes the lingering night so cling to thee?" or "Canyon Marvellous, / The secret of thy stillness lies unveiled / In wordless worship!"—addresses some of the same themes that other poets do, but with words that a contemporary audience would consider over-the-top romanticism, if not parody.

We brought the same guiding questions to the hundreds of contemporary canyon poems that we read. Here the task was harder. The majority rang with the currency of common words used well, and with the authenticity of having been conceived on site, and we remain grateful for the privilege of reading every single poem sent us by our fellow canyon enthusiasts. Our final decisions were based on our judgment of which poems invited us to think about the canyon from fresh perspectives, and how each poem contributed to the wide-ranging conversation that the book became. Many voices infuse this chorus: Hopi and Navajo and Anglos; river-runners and hikers and dwellers at the rim; rangers and geologists and teachers and painters—poets all, an assemblage of individuals who succeed, despite Cobb's claim, in "getting away with the job." It is our hope that their words will prove true companions on your own Grand Canyon journey, whether you are on the river, the trail, the rim, or elsewhere, yearning to return.

References

Cobb, Irvin S. *Roughing It De Luxe*. Philadelphia: The Curtis Publishing Company, 1913.

Dutton, Clarence E. *Tertiary History of the Grand Cañon District*. Tucson: University of Arizona, 2001.

Gerke, Sarah Bohl and Paul Hirt. "Nature, Culture, and History at the Grand Canyon: Literature." Arizona State University. Web. 9 March 2013.

Hughes, Donald J. *The Story of Man at the Grand Canyon*. Grand Canyon Natural History Association, 1972.

Lamb, Susan, editor. *The Best of Grand Canyon Nature Notes*. Grand Canyon Natural History Association, 1994.

Powell, J.W. *The Exploration of the Colorado River and Its Canyons*. New York: Dover, 1961.

Pyne, Stephen J. *How the Canyon Became Grand*. New York: Viking Penguin, 1998.

Van Dyke, John Charles. *The Grand Canyon of the Colorado: Recurrent Studies in Impressions and Appearances*. New York: Charles Scribner's Sons, 1920.

ON THE RIM

Introducing Others to the Edge
Thea Gavin

Mortals: meet
the empty air,
arias carved
out of rocks beyond
our puny clock
philosophy.

Venerable cleft
in the Kaibab Plateau:
these are my friends.
Treat them as well as
you've treated me—
burn their muscles,
scar their skin
and memory.

Grand Canyon
Joan Baranow

You have come to the edge in your T-shirt and tennis shoes,
the trail map snapping in the sudden wind, and there,

like nothing you had imagined, nothing
in the pocket-sized postcards or the travelers' guides,

is the split continent, enormous and jagged,
a terrible incision, terribly gorgeous,

the late-afternoon air pouring in
like liquid spilled from far fissures or glacial thaw.

Below, invisible, is the green wiry river
rubbing against rock, pursuing its prehistoric task.

You'd not expected such a vast accident,
your shock the same as seeing a live heart

beating, or the blood of a baby's birth.
Soon you'll descend, shouldering a pack

down switchback trails into the open wound,
where, at dawn, you crawl from your nylon tent

to watch the sun, that rusty, iron ball,
hurl itself over the broken earth.

At the Grand Canyon
Fred Dings

Clouds float like islands in the river of air
which flows between the walls. The Colorado,

a sliver of water, glints at the bottom like a knife.
Ephemeral as fruit flies, airplanes flit

among the cliffs, while laden mules labor
down to a present millions of years below.

On the edge of the gouge, herds of awed tourists
gape at the immense ruined rainbows of time.

"I wish I could live here," someone says,
not noticing the clutch of desert plants

struggling at his feet, which soon will die
and blow across the stones, stain the rocks,

or lodge as molecules of dust in someone's eye.
How much grandeur does it take until

our eyes fall to the small life before us,
the geologic blink we call our lives,

how long before we settle on a few roots
finding life in a handful of burning sand,

keeping their grip inside the wind which whistles
faintly as it whets against their limbs?

The Lens Frames this Image
Margaret Randall

The lens frames this image
then lets it go
as I slowly sweep walls
that move in the opposite direction
faster than my camera
can do its work.

Panning space but also time:
centuries of buildup,
millennia of sedimentation,
uplift, intrusion, deposit,
erosion, faulting
and the shudder of tectonic plates.

I want to hold the shadow
of an instant gone
two hundred million years ago,
its movement
playing across my line of vision.

I would register this shift of earth,
the roar of boulders
hurtling down a tributary,
the power of pink granite
slicing schist.

I know the camera keeps out
more than it lets in,
obscures more than it reveals.
Only when I lower the Nikon
and free my eye
does light explode
in that crescent of rock,

will darkness creep up
from the deepest slot,
walls claiming one color
and then another
until full circumference
whispers the password
and I move through.

The Colors of Darkness
Chana Bloch

Rothko Chapel, Houston

Flash after flash across the horizon:
tourists trying to take the Grand Canyon
by night. They don't know
every last shot will turn out black.

It takes Rothko sixty years to arrive
at the rim of his canyon.
He goes there only after dark.
As he stands at the railing, his pupils open
like a camera shutter at the slowest speed.

He has to be patient. He has to lean
far over the railing
to see the colors of darkness:
purple, numb brown, mud-red, mauve
—an abyss of bruises.
At first, you'd think it was black-on-black.
"Something you don't want to look at," he says.

As he waits,
the colors vibrate in the chasm
like voices:
            You there with the eyes,
bring back something from
the brink of nothing
to make us see.

Thomas Moran Paints
Daniel Williams

This place gets inside you with its soft reds
And tans   you can feel the lithe sweep of brushes
Inside your head   your empty hands moving
From side to side involuntarily   It is like seeing
An angel's brilliancy for the first time and trying
To describe it to your own soul in a language
Of the eye your heart can understand
The light is always different here getting darker
Near the river   paler near the rim   but it is
The way the canyon breathes warm air rising
Cool air settling that makes the colors vibrant
Gives them luster   I can pile and scrape paint
On a canvass forever and miss the one rare
Note that hides in the throat of a canyon wren
But I can dream that bird within me and capture
It on silk where its song will bring this magical
Secret landscape into my art on its wings

Grand Canyon/West
Mary Beath

Human stories roll across the
landscape, demanding attention, voicing
their energy, responding to my questions;
the land only vibrates in the wind.
Or not. Rocks and lava, caught in the moment
of fall, of flow, expose fractured
innards and cooled heat, vibrate only rarely.
These human voices and the tales they tell
deflect with their looks, their gestures,
their act of giving me what I can feel
myself, or at least understand. I can't
put myself in the piñon's place, trembling at
the edge, growing at the upper end of a
human-sized bowl, the lower end a slot I peer
through to see the river's ribbon, its white-flecked
trail through the deepest cleft of all. I can't
know the piñon's mind, though I try.
These tales from another's mouth make sense,
but spread a thin veneer over all the
rest. Still, the distraction is never
irredeemable: the human voices go, the wind
comes forward again, blows the chittering,
zooming swifts; the piñon watches the same
stretch of river through its rock cleft,
watches the tiny rafts with their human cargo
pass beneath it, all stories quieted,
distance far too deep.

Sunrise, Grand Canyon
John Barton

We stand on the edge, the fall
into depth, the ascent

of light revelatory, the canyon walls moving
up out of

shadow, lit
colours of the layers cutting

down through darkness, sunrise as it
passes a

precipitate of the river, its burnt tangerine
flare brief, jagged

bleeding above the far rim for a split
second I have imagined

you here with me, watching day's onslaught
standing in your bones—they seem

implied in the record almost
by chance—fossil remains held

in abundance in the walls, exposed
by freeze and thaw, beautiful like a theory stating

who we are is
carried forward by the x

chromosome down the matrilineal line
recessive and riverine, you like

me aberrant and bittersweet, and losing
your hair just when we have begun

to know the limits of beauty, you so
distant from me now but at ease

in a chair in your kitchen, pensive, mind
wandering away from yesterday's *Times*, the ink

rubbing off on your hands, dermatoglyphic
and telltale, but unread

on the chair arms after you
had pushed yourself to your feet such

a while ago, I'd say, for here I am
three hours behind you, riding the high

Colorado Plateau as the opposing
continental plates force it over

a mile upward without buckling, smooth
tensed, muscular fundament, your bones yet

to be wrapped around mine—
this will come later, when I return

to your place and time, I know it, you not
ready for past or future, our combined

bones so inconsequent yet
personal, the geo

logic cross
section of the canyon dropping

from where I stand, hundreds
millions of shades of terra cotta, of copper

manganese and rust, the many varieties of stone—
silt, sand, and slate, even "green

river rock," a rough misidentified
fragment of it once unknowingly

dropped when I was a boy into my as-of-yet
unsettled sediments by a man who tried

to explain how slowly the Earth meta
morphosed from my meagre

Wolf Cub's collection of rocks, his sheer
casual physicality enough to negate

all received wisdom, my body voicing its immense
genetic imperatives, human

geology falling away
into a

depth I am still unprepared for
the canyon cutting down to

the great unconformity, a layer
so named by the lack

of any fossil evidence to hypothesize
about and date such

a remote time by, at last no possible
retrospective certainties, what a

relief, your face illegible
these words when I began not what I had

intended to say—something new about
the natural dynamic between

earth and history, beauty and art—
but you are my subject, unavoidable

and volatile, the canyon
floor a mile from where I objectively

stand taking photos I will later develop of
the ripe, trans

formative light on these surreal
buttes to show you on the surface

how beautiful and diverse
and unimportant our time together

or with anyone else
really is—

Grand Canyon Cowboy
S. Omar Barker

I'd heard of the Canyon (the old cowboy said)
And I figured I'd like to go see it.
So I rode till I sighted a rim out ahead,
And reckoned that this place might be it.

I anchored my horse to a juniper limb
And crawled to the edge for a peek.
One look was a plenty to make my head swim.
And all of my innards feel weak.

If I'd known how durned deep it was going to be,
I'd have managed, by some hook or crook,
To tie my ownself to the doggoned tree
And let my horse go take the look!

Death in the Grand Canyon
Ryn Gargulinski

this one was frozen in a gully
this one had tumbled from the
brink—that one was found
near his water face down as
some voices told him not to drink

this one was swept in a
flash flood—this one was
blanched by the sun—that one
went far in his very fast car that
had sped to its very last run

this one was drowned in the
river—this one was crushed
by big stones—that one don't
know how he happened to go
all that's left is a pile of bones

this one was posing for a
photo—this one veered way
off his course—and that
one was shoved by a
husband out of love as it's
cheaper than
getting a
divorce.

Grand Canyon National Park
Michael Kabotie

"Mike, look at how
pretty the canyon is!"
                    Frances shouted

"I can't look, I'm driving;
besides I will make my
final journey
to the underworld
through the sipapuni,"
                    I answered

A spiritual place
our symbolic womb-kiva
the place of emergence
through which we
enter our underworld
                    heaven

"The Grand Canyon
discovered in 1540
by Pedro de Cardenas"
                    The National Parks pamphlet read

I smiled
knowing that my people
always knew
the Grand Canyon was there
and didn't need to be discovered

Cardenas came with
Hopi guides and
I learned how lies
are twisted to sound
                    true

But on my final journey
I promised to stop at all

the sight-seeing points
to mingle with the tourists
                and
give them my last earthly
trinkets before I descend
into my
                            eternal womb/kiva.

Sometimes She Dreams
Laura Tohe

This woman
I call my mother
quit school in her teens to follow
                her Grand Canyon dreams
                where she dreams of becoming
more than maid, waitress, cook, wife.

As the bus races down the smooth highway
the magazine falls open on her lap and she fills
in her name on the white card to the
                "LaSalle Extension School of Law---
                Learn law at home in your spare time."
But she never sends it.

Through the shiny reflection of the glass window
she sees the wooden billboards along Highway 66 near Lupton,
"See Real Indians Inside Making Jewelry, Weaving rugs."

This isn't what her mother wanted
but she seems destined to follow the same highway
her mother took to a kitchen in California
where the dishes rattled in their cupboards.

The bus stops in front of the big hotel
where she later stripped and tightened the bed covers
after the tourists left.
And outside the Canyon stretched wide her arms
                the way her dreams must have felt
                back then,
                wide and open,
                        so much space to be filled.

Along the Widforss Trail
Jean Rukkila

In the woods,
lightning-struck survivors
don't tell their stories.
You don't hear a tree
hissing as you go by,
I was damaged once.
Lightning-struck trees
stand unmoved.
With a renewed interest
in their roots, perhaps.
How all those tendrils
held onto fistfuls of earth
while light shattered through.
How cells gasped,
a sound sent out for miles
by billions of pine needles,
a whole afternoon's whispering
compressed into a millisecond,
and amplified
when lightning flashes.
But no storytelling.
And yet a story glows,
electric history
caught in the bark
of the pine
with a spiral scar.

Is it the tough heart
that keeps a tree standing
while others shatter?
Or is it the liquid heart,
the spirit cauldron meeting heat
drawing up the loud present,
shivering with love
for explosive now.

Fall Dispersal
Thea Gavin

Oct. 15, 2011
For the North Rim seasonal crew

"Aerial dispersal appears to be stimulated
by overcrowding and food shortage,
and also by a physiological need to move
to new habitats at a certain stage
in the life cycle of some species."
-Eric Duffey, "Aerial dispersal in spiders"

Filaments—the air is
hung with lazy curve and sway.
Over the canyon
these evening glints
call: fling yourself into the still—
you will twist
a bit and float
and fall upon
the breath of red layers
releasing the day's warmth, carrying you out—
there—free as canyon light,
drifty as canyon shadow,
catching eventually.

Eating Fruit at the Grand Canyon—
A Song to Make Death Easy
Diana Hume George

Since this great hole in earth is beyond
my comprehension and I am hungry,
I sit on the rim and eat fruit

the colors of the stone I see,
strawberries of iron cliffs, sagebrush
melons, whitesand apple, grapes

the barely purple of the stonewashed slopes,
and every color I eat is in my vision,
colonized by my eye, by me and everyone

I have known, so vast, remote,
that we can only gaze at ourselves, wondering
at our reaches, eat fat fruit while we

grow calm if we can, our folded
rocky interiors pressed upwards through
our throats, side canyons seeming almost

accessible, the grand river of blood
carving us even as we sit, devouring
color that will blush on our skin,

nourish us so that we may climb
the walls of the interior, bewildered,
tremulous, but observant as we move

down in, one foot, another,
careful not to fall, to fall,
the fruit fueling us in subtle

surges of color in this vasty deep
where birds make shadow and echo
and we have no idea

why we cannot comprehend ourselves,
each other, a place so deep and bright
it has no needs, and we wonder

what we're doing here on this fragment
of galactic dust, spinning, cradled,
awestruck, momentarily alive.

A Coyote Runs Across My Path at Midnight
in the Pine Loop Campground at Grand Canyon
Carol Henrie

If you drink your tea by the light
gnats and mosquitoes dive in
and drown, but if you drink in the dark
you might swallow something you failed
to see. We cook in this night,
autumn humming nearer, ants and opalescent
beetles gathering stores fallen
from our meal. Summer and we summer people
use everything, the very air. Water
sleeps in the rocks here and the taps
trickle over soapy plates,
the forks we pack away. We cook
with melted ice from the cooler. All day
we watched hawks and ravens
give themselves like children
to the arms of air. I touched my daughter's
hair, it hurt my throat
to see the miles of space between
that soaring and its shadow.

Something wakes me, singing
at a distant fire, something cold
pressed against my back through cotton duck
and down, sharp as teeth and unexpected
as the kitten's needle bite. Deep
in the rock a shelf of ice
splintering me from sleep as if
a storm had torn the night
and I fell in. The tent a dome
over a sullen desert and its own
drab sky. My foot on the path,
the city of sleeping campers in their
blue tents, red tents, like a field of tulips.
Stars, stars, point of view: I can feel
light on my shoulders like a shawl,
civilizing my hair, when the first coyote
lopes across my path in the circle

of light, smiling over her shoulder. Wouldn't I be an enlightened woman if I were star-blessed every night? The second coyote saunters by and does not notice me at all.

Grand Canyon of the Colorado
Bill Holm

This big emptiness is the hollow under
your bed at three years old where something
too fast for light waits to chew at you.

It's the hole under the pasture that cows
know about before a tornado. At night,
there's an invisible river a mile underfoot.

Watch the tourists, brave with cameras
at sundown, cowering away from the silence
flooding up at them through the dark.

Here we're all children waiting on a branch
for the sound of something climbing up
from the hole nothing should ever get out of.

The Silence, The Sun
Phyllis Hoge Thompson

The silence is simpler,
deeper even than the abyss
the Colorado
coursing through Arizona
graved into rock,

hangs weightless
everywhere
confounding thought,

buries the canyon
beneath the sun
comprehending all of it,

broods.
Even the river's water-thunder
does not rise to the rim.

All the blind hours
sun chronicles shadows
sloping over steeps of Earth

here
where centuries come together
still
uncounted
in the silence
which does not tell.

The Grand Canyon
Maynard Dixon

When I look at this great solid Earth
And think how measurelessly old it is—
The layered rocks burnt black with ancient fires
Laid down and cut by lost receding seas,
And see the little stunted pines that march
The canyon's brink, that grow the same to-day,
And shed their little cones into the abyss,
As when the first vague giant emperors
Of China ruled,—yes, ages yet beyond—
The same to-day;—I wonder where's the use
To agitate rebellion?—Nations—Art?—
What are they? And what difference does it make
Whether this man is crippled, or that wife is true?
The warm immediate commands of life,—
Moist touch of passion—the relief of tears,
The microscopic labors we perform,—
The fluctuating borders of our time,—
The half-known movements of a century,
The growth of races building from beneath. . . .
Cut through like colored layers in the rock,
High over which the moving Spirit sweeps,
A giant wind along the canyon's rim.

Entering Temples of Silence
James Hart

> *"The prudent keep silent."*
> *-John Muir*

This should be the holy canyon
of the silent world, the airy crossroads
where speechless pilgrims pause, edges
of something eternities older than God.
My son who likes to measure his world
in fractions and precise percentages
tells me seven out of ten voices
we hear speak in foreign tongues,
and someday he'll realized this chasm
opens a fraction of time's immortality.
Flocks of Asians in dark-winged hair
cluster at overlooks, chatter language
as alien as Anasazi to me as they pose
for ubiquitous Kodak moments where
Zoroaster's temple mutely pierces time,
mysteriously distant in morning haze,
a rugged backdrop for day's ragged fray,
tourist herds pushing ultimate views.
Eventually, this international babble
rises, disappears to meaningless air
as ravens drop from rimless cliffs,
the canyon's black keepers of silence
opening wings on ancient updrafts
to glide peerlessly into granite past
opened before us. This planet's wound,
the red flesh of eons, offers a healing
balm, pale temples, muted towers,
forgotten waters whispering vast
tongues of void too great to contain
the echoes of any human language.

Field Trip: Grand Canyon, North Rim
David Lee

> *What we observe is not nature itself, but nature exposed to our method of questioning.*
> —*Werner Heisenberg*

"Therefore, students, the air I breathe here, then, is relative and quantum: an abstract entity with dual aspect, which falls away into the place I call distance, which I intuit. As the sound of the river rises, particles move in frequencies proportional to their energies, which, scientifically, is air in the cavity of the gorge resonating with the speed of its vibration, produced by imposition of orderly alternations of compression and decompression, referred to as waves, on the natural order of the distribution of the molecules of the air, which is the opposite of the natural state of disorder, or entropy, in which the molecules usually exist, unless energy is applied to force them into the more ordered state. This energy, then, is released, or better, transferred, by the action of gravity, a force, on the mass of the river's water, impacting the rocks, the water, any existing flora, and the waves themselves. The water remains unseen, the canyon cradling it in its distance is translated as depth, held in place by gravity. The river flows westward through space, not separate but intimately connected with time, which forms a four-dimensional continuum curved by mass. Beyond the near distance the red wall of the south rim rises from the absence which is presence invisible, innumerable photons racing before the eye at the speed of light, its mass nothing more than a form of energy, the red wall not a static object but a vigorously charged pattern, a process involving the energy which manifests itself as the particle's unified body, computed by multiplying that mass by the speed of light squared, the space about it bent, its curvature depending on the physical volume of the object, time as well affected by its presence, flowing at a different rate through different matter in different temporal sequences, the entire structure of space-time depending on the distribution of matter in the universe which is, then, finally and ultimately, a dynamic, organic, inseparable entity which always includes the observer in an essential way."

A man in green walking shorts, black socks, and brown wingtip shoes stands beside me, staring into the canyon. His legs above his socks are very white. I suspect he has come here for vacation, probably with his family who did not wish to walk the quarter-mile distance to the point. We do not speak. I do not look at his face. He turns, moves away, and we part like deer in an immutable forest. Beyond the south rim the far distance bends into horizon, fades into pale blue sky with its tatters of white cirrus clouds, falling away like breath.

from Many Hats
Carl Sandburg

On the rim a quizzical gray-glinting hombre was telling himself how it looked to him—the sun and the air are endless with silver tricks—the light of the sun has crimson stratagems—the changes go on in stop-watch split seconds—the blues slide down a box of yellow and mix with reds that melt into gray and come back saffron clay and granite pink—a weaving gamble of color twists on and it is anybody's guess what is next.

A long sand-brown shawl shortens to a glimmering turquoise scarf—as the parapets and chimneys wash over and out in the baths of the sunset and the floats of the gloaming, one man says, There goes God with an army of banners, and another man, Who is God and why? who am I and why?

> He told himself, This may be
> something else than what I
> see when I look—how do I
> know? For each man sees him-
> self in the Grand Canyon—
> each one makes his own Canyon
> before he comes, each one brings
> and carries away his own Canyon—
> who knows? and how do I know?

This World
Ken Lauter

> *We hear that other lands are better; we do not know.*
> *The pines sing and we are glad. Our children play*
> *in the sand; we hear them sing and are glad. The seeds*
> *ripen and we have [them] to eat and we are glad.*
> *We do not want their good lands; we want our*
> *rocks and the great mountains where our fathers lived.*
> *-a Shi'vwits chief to J.W. Powell*

Sun on redrock
ravens riding thermals
jays crazy in the pines

big blue mountain
on the far horizon
and here: *infinite air—*

moving, opening
east-west, north-south,
up-down, high

over the one-way river
pulling
the whole sky west.

What need
for any other world?

A Winter Day at Grand Canyon
William Wallace Bass

The gentle lights of morningtime
       Gave color to a cloud
While in the Canyon down below
       Some sunlight was allowed.

Rays filtering through the overcast
       Came from the rising sun
Slanting inward from the east
       The day had just begun.

I walked beneath a snow-clad roof
       The Lookout was not far
Beyond a hanging icicle
       Was Hotel El Tovar.

Through branches of a sprawling bush
       Encased in ice and snow
I saw bright sun on upper wall
       Which fell to cliff below.

Then suddenly right at my feet
       Snow crystals glistened bright
While the abyss below the Rim
       Was still as dark as night.

Bright Angel Canyon now was clear
       But clouds were hanging low
And in the foreground could be seen
       The river gorge plateau.

Then just as swiftly as it came
       The sunlight went away
The clouds had closed in overhead
       But not for long to stay.

For soon some highlights did appear
       The sun was coming through

Striking first down in the depths
 Then high on Temple Manu.

A golden glow lit up the walls
 Along Bright Angel Creek
Like fantasy in Fairyland
 Of others worlds to speak.

And then our Canyon pageantry
 Put on another show
I saw it wholly clothed in white
 All blanketed with snow.

Exquisite clouds came floating by
 Some formed before my eyes
Within the depths of canyon walls
 A magic beauty lies.

Dark shadow came o'er all the land
 Complete from rim to rim
The grandeur there could still be seen
 Although the light was dim.

Now Cheops pyramid was to be
 Finale of the show
From Heaven came a shaft of light
 More color to bestow.

Upon its rugged shapely crest
 With terraced clouds below
The glory of this magic hour
 No man again will know.

No words of man, by tongue or pen
 Can e'er this scene convey
To anyone who missed the show
 This wondrous winter day.

Sentry Duty at the Canyon
Dorothy Brooks

Sinuous as a brush stroke
the red rock unfolds,

holds down the ribbon river.
It knows

who its lovers are: those
of us who must leave—

those with the patience of ants
and the certitude

of squirrels—that we will return,
one by one. We'll

come back to the claret light
the moon splaying

on the stretched silence
and the great gash

that the layered mesas guard.

The Grand Canyon
Stephen Lefebure

As if there were instead some limit
To this world which follows where we go;
As if we could renounce the many
Habits we acquired long ago;
As if we could embrace the infinite
Spaces we traverse like falling snow;
Or as if we ourselves had any
Substance, and were present; even so,
Just when we are ready to admit
Defeat we find ourselves on this plateau
Staring out across long violet
Reaches filling up with indigo.

Ballad of the Bright Angel
Bruce Berger

> *O happy horse, to bear the weight of Antony!*
> *—Shakespeare*

Jammed into denim, grinning in Polaroid,
Sneakers and tote bags banging, they lurch and sway
Through Paleozoic sandstone, overjoyed
To be out of their vans at last and chafing their way
Down the ages of the Grand Canyon, and every day
Their mouths are cinched with some new cross to carry.
Only guide and steed are hitched to stay.
O happy mule, to bear the weight of Jerry.

Neck-stroking co-eds, machos loudly annoyed
To be stuck near the rear, matrons who must weigh
More than the chuck box, snake phobics even Freud
Would buck from the couch, equestrians hot to display
Inappropriate talents, students of Zane Grey
Who holler *whoa!* and *giyyup!* in accents that vary
From Youngstown to Stockholm to Dallas to Mandalay—
O happy mule, to bear the weight of Jerry!

Kicking their rental beasts along the void,
Pummeling soft ears with a ceaseless bray
Of past excursions, pizza, paranoid
State troopers, smartphones, prices in Santa Fe
And the world's most adorable grandchildren, are they
En Route to Phantom Ranch or Canterbury?
Who cares with apple cores for overpay?
O happy mule, to bear the weight of Jerry!

Envoi

Fred Harvey, it's a tacky crowd today.
O happy hand, to team up with the very
Jewel of your help that runs on hay.
And happy Jewel, to bear the weight of Jerry!

Grand Canyon
Mark Irwin

Red rock
Sheered by the sun's
Drizzling rays; a steeped haze drops, descends
¾'s of a mile
Into the smoky blue
Shade. Down

We move
Through a thousand runneled buttes,
Eroded Byzantiums
Of red-ignited
Sandstone and shale. Pinnacles and minarets
Flame; towers, arches, domes
Dissolve into shadowy plateaus. To the east,

Bruise-blue,
Vishnu's Temple and Wotan's Throne
Support the sky. Above, the putty-white colonnades
—Osiris, Isis—shine.

The canyon walls balloon
With light. Clouds,

Cumulus, drag
Brief lakes of shade.
Purples avalanche grey
Into the inner
Gorge. Down,

Leveling out now
Onto the Tonto Plain,
Its dead sea floor a grey
Reptile head. Cremation
Creek's a pulp of
Dust; heat

Floods up. No
Sound. The last
Sunclad rocks, a skink
Freezes on stone. The sky

Indigo drowsed gold, a jet's
Contrail, the first
Narcotic stars. A cocooned stillness
Tugs us on. Listening
Like children in the storydusk,
We descend toward the river's
Green tongue.

Going Down Grand
Danny Rosen

Canyon rock. Hard
going down, down
by layer, down by grain,
down under thunder-named:
Kaibab, Toroweap, Coconino
Sandstone. Switching back
to shale, toenail turning
black, rock red and raw,
soft color and far—walking
down rattled, humping, high-
stepping, hurting at the knee,
bending to the wind, contouring
round, counting down the lines,
four-legging landslides—crumbling
and steep, down karst, down travertine.
Sipping Muav seep.
                    Sundown at Supai
sunk down the esplanade sky.
Red-walled allegiance vanished down
a blue carbon stream; satellites flare,
scorpions creep.

Rising to rock: towers, uplifts, buried
hogbacks, slumped blocks, exposed
folds—cracked and monoclined.
Flat-lined gaps of time—eroded wide,
raven-eyed, white-throated,
red-budded, big-horned, fossilized.
Planetary yellow-bush hillside, slanting
from young Sun. Walking-Down-Man: out Tonto
legging long, thinking down, looking in, hiding out
in the shade. Raven gets a lizard. Century stalks
win, place, show, lay down, melt in the haze. Shade
on shade, buff on pink, green on gray, gray ridge
on a gray ridge day, fade and fade and fade away.

Down to a bright angel, down to black,
down to brown, down to still, unconforming,
uncaring slot of chasm time: dark, cold, polished
to glass stone, cooling slowly in. Black striped by white,
Vishnu shot by a burning dyke, crushing in, breaking down
to me now laying on rock taking its heat, dying slow by the river.

Reaching Rider Canyon
Bruce Berger

Half-droused, you stumble your way
Through sage, hard sand,
Rubble, noon and pure sky,
And the bottom drops. A cold wind
Sings through your bones and space
Enters. A few more pitted feet
Of rock shield you from absence,
Then sandstone sheers straight
To murderous talus, past
The dry streambed and back up the far
Dark wall to a mirror of where you are.
It's like being knocked out
In a dream, or maybe a pulse
Of what gulps beyond the last
Breath, when no body rises to meet
The loosened sense, and you can't tell
Yet if you're fixed for flight,
Or there's anywhere to fall.

Upper Ribbon Falls
Andrea Ross

Cottonwood surrenders its smoky wisps in this canyon,
my cracking body merely a holding place, empty granary
in a heat-mirrored cliff. The nearby waterfall's conversation—
regret, regret, regret—slaps across chalky sandstone the way
a trapped moth's wings rise against cupped hands. Light and wind
pollinate this canyon, and solitude glitters in the creek bed
like a familiar face. What is given? What taken? Does oblivion
swim these shallows? An old trail stumps alongside the stream,
its time-burned rocks placed like bricks inside this strip of earth,
this tiny vessel of chattering leaves. Flared sky gropes through
the Mesozoic's deep belly, breaking apart—breaking and freezing,
burning and cracking with the smoldering question:

> "Whose body is this?"

Walk All Day
Philip Wofford

Walk all day
In the same place
In a gorge so deep
The sky is narrow
As a line of blue thread.

And at night
Lie down where you started
And count the same stars
Until the sun rises again
Revealing where you always were.

Then, walk another day
In the same place
In a gorge so deep
The sky is narrow
As a line of blue thread.

Tonto Plateau, Grand Canyon
Reg Saner

What on earth have I done with today?
Watched 5 AM buttes lose weight
and gain color. Later, near flowering stalks
of agave, saw humongous black bees
fumbling pollen from blooms
all but too rich for them. Then
shaded by overhang,
watched ravens ride thermals
high above collared lizards flexing forelegs.

Among rains resurrected as cactus
I confessed to a great river: "No need to mind me,
just say whatever you said long before this
when there was no one to hear it."

So, where time and the land
wear the same face I listened all afternoon
and in the hustle, then whisper, then roar,
then whisper again, heard the world
falling forever away from the world
and in the river's voice the sound
of always, pouring, pouring
through everything we believe.

The Geologist
Michael Blumenthal

Grand Canyon, Arizona, May 1988

He had made a life of stone:
of sandstone and basalt,
of dolomite and shale
and the wild permutations of schist.
Siltstones spoke to him
and the hard crystals of metamorphic rock:
His life became a history
of sediments and erosions,
of deep strata fissured and faulted
into a great transmutation
of flakes and erabering chips.
Nights, he spoke in his sleep
of downcutting rivers,
primordial sea floors
crumpled and forced into islands,
only to resubmerge as wandering continents.
He could see the veins of magma
shooting up through the mountain ranges,
he could feel the great unconformities,
the missing pages and sentences
of subsidences and diastems.
All that he loved of the world
was stone and water, water and wind,
Cambrian and Paleozoic. But he was not
a stupid man, by any stretch
of the imagination. For he never mistook
pyrite for true gold. He was not fool enough
ever to take gneiss for granite.

The Great Unconformity
Rebecca Lawton

—*after E.D. McKee*

Fifteen thousand feet
are gone: the sea broken off
        gaps open between strata
        entire islands lost
under drifting sands
When you stop to rest
you know millennia
may still surface. Quartzite
cuts your thighs—you find
sandstone unforgiving
The break in record,
regained, would speak
more than entire
dissertations. What made you

think you'd be the one
to stand in the missing eras
        with no sign, perhaps
        one hundred million years gone
and tell their story? No lifetime
spent sifting through papers
can be reclaimed, no more
than the eons it took
to build mountains
will return

There is absence
        beveled schists
        stolen history
where guidebooks say to look
Your place in
the Great Unconformity
has slipped out of memory
the way the layers

resting on upturned rocks
clearly preserved elsewhere
remain mute on your life

from Who Are You, Grand Canyon?
Yevgeny Yevtushenko

A young girl descends to the Colorado River.
About sixteen.
She is so delighted,
sleeping gear juts out of her rucksack.
She looks about unearthly,
heavenly.
A dog on a safety leash
pulls her
along the edge of the abyss.
This tourist is a little different:
she has no fear of the deadly risk,
she has no desire to cling to the shadows.
She moves strangely,
stepping cautiously.
Shudder, Grand Canyon:
she is blind.
Let not a tiny stone strike her.
Quietly she moves on the leash above the river,
touching the sky with her free hand,
caressing tenderly the clouds with her cheeks
in the morning hour.
On her face so many freckles—
childlike all-seeing eyes!
Greedily gulping the air
her skin sees
the Grand Canyon,
the miracle of its beauty.
And wounded by its healing beauty,
a blind girl
down in the Grand Canyon
is,
Grand Canyon,
above you.

A Grand Canyon Suite
Carol Kanter

I. Moon

Her single whole note hovers
haunts thin air in white face
deep-set gray eyes reflecting
little light. Seductive,
she peels the dark from midnight,
floods the earth in opal,
her leitmotifs played high…
low…high…as she sidles
along the tight-rope of night
stretched between the walls' full stops.

II. Walls

A stack of cosmic secrets
centuries thick—codified
at sundown by choruses
of crickets, frogs, night-guarded
by wink-owls, dive-bomber bats;
while days, the great blue heron
shifts from leg to leg, alone,
opening its wings to span
low the purple shadow space
where dragonflies surf the wind.

III. River

An endless sound track runs
southwest to play smooth jazz
along the pebbly edge,
to thunder-roar mid-stream,
and where calm meets rapid
to eddy in rondos—
while beneath, bass currents
saw on like a cellist
practicing long, open G's
that deepen water's bed

IV. Tributary

Giggling, flirty fast, the brook
kicks up a gigue, elbows flecks
of crystal sun to scamper
from wavelet to wavelet...
until a mainstream rush
quenches her sprightly fun,
or a sudden storm whips
her into swells that douse
her come-on lights, roil her
a steep and murky brown.

V. Rocks

Lopped off boulders litter
the canyon floor, soak up
daytime desert rays, glow
white with heat, too sizzly
for those lacking lizard skin
to lean against for more
than one hot second; nights,
each rough-hewn, porous kiln
out-radiates the whole moon's
lonely, stone-cold watch.

VI. Agave

Only once in seven years
the desert agave blooms—
shoots up tall a strong plump stalk
whose garish petals glitter
as if the very violet light
that tanned to monochrome
the shore's dry sand, burnished it
with syncopated gold leaf.
Cache these riches in
before they tarnish,
                    crumble,

waft.

Alchemy
Ann Weiler Walka

Old knees absorb the terrain,
The pitch and texture—rotting shale,
Limestone edges, cobbles
Poised to roll underfoot—
And eyes and nose the local flora—
Stunted and spiny or wind twisted
Or perfumed and delicate
As any hot house flower—
And ears long damped
Against civilization reopen
To raven whoosh and bee thrum.

Arriving at the river sore and happy
We celebrate our initiation
Into this lower world
With sardines and
Sips of Irish whiskey.

It's later though in my skinny bed,
The ground adrift and the moon and
The water noodling lullabies,
That the sky pours into me
And the vast distance
Between here and up there.
By morning I have no other home.

FROM THE RIVER

River Run
Rita Maria Magdaleno

> *...you will know the loss*
> *of guile and that the journey*
> *has begun.*
>   *-Barry Lopez, River Notes*

Among the mesas and soft
lavender hills, there is
silence, birds circling
in spirals of light
and forgiveness.

Out there in the hills,
juniper laces the land,
a nickel moon shining,
smell of sagebrush
and sand creeping
into our bones.

There, the ice-edged
night will begin to fall
away, a cloudless sky
bright with stars.

At dawn, we will enter
water, begin to speak
the names of river places:
Crystal Rapid, Lava
Falls, Havasu Creek.

There, an arbor of cottonwood
and willow will gather
in the distance, and
small fish will breathe
beneath our boat, flicker
of gills, glisten of fins
and oars—first
run, the joy
we bear.

Erosional
Thorpe Moeckel

Motion of torso & oar.
                              Flowmotions.
Later, the Vishnu schist.
Feeling thorny? Or

has that baggage boat you're rowing
got the goods
                    from the groover?
Nothing's airtight in these waves.
Forget Ha Na Na Wash,

Havasupai,
The Great Unconformity—hear
what being small can explore

you into. Something

of allness. And none. Zoical.
What era is this?
                    What upwelling
sucks the Chubb? Pull.

This pool. Then waves, a good
tongue—one move,
                    angle right &
pull, miss the pour-over (see it

sound the insides,
time's). You can't forget. Ouzel in

& out some
sidecreek curtain. Havasu's jazz &
blues. Cliffleap. Tamarisk,
yucca. Camp three, ten, six. Moon

half-rimmed below

Nankoweap. Hackysack, sandal-tan.
Granaries.
              All dams leak.

from Canyon Notes
Beth Paulson

How to understand *river*:
ride eight days on its back
between walls time carved a mile deep
rose blood-red gray-green black—
not yet speaking its language
give it words
swift-running silt-laden shimmering.

Mornings wake to mud-colored riffles
where current surge and splash
wet shirts to flesh shivers—
afternoons dream in still places
skin hot in sweaty drowse

until dusk shades the river platinum
its rush muffled by cool sand
where pink tamarisk grow
like feathers among boulders
and sacred datura open
diaphanous as moths
where at night moonlight rides
on ripples cast with uncountable stars.

Sanctuary
Seth Muller

Sanctuary begins
in tree-shade, by water,
in the envelope of canyon—

in the pockets of erosion
where the devil wind
cannot invade.

Rock frames sky.
Thoughts yield
to elements.
Veins of leaves
create the only maps.

The fragrance of rabbitbrush
draws a traffic of insects.
What lives can congregate.

Sand keeps missives,
soon erased. And we
cannot stay.

Fence Fault
Heidi Elizabeth Blankenship

Ravens watch
from the rocks.
A lady bug drops
from a tree.
Frigid green rapids
snap at stony edges.
What more can we give to this world?
Nothing but walking
here softly,
with our hearts
wide open to beauty,
with our eyes
catching rainbows
and shadows.
Downstream from the condors
perched at Navajo Bridge,
we offer our footsteps
on sandy river banks
peppered with willows
gently tossing
their long heads
near the Redwall spring
screaming with yellow
monkey flowers.

Along Rockfall
Steve Wilson

At the heart of the canyon, along rockfall,
dry stream and limestone caves: the echoed call

of a hawk. Shrub oaks, lowed, grow here,
fed on the fractured light. Whisper-clear,
this flow of sun over sheer stones. Near
dry stream and limestone caves, the echoed call

that settles into the darknesses between
boulders. Even in the smallest crevice, green
growth. Lichen, extravagant as coral, and lean,
at the heart of the canyon, along rockfall,

shows itself, has its say where only we know.
Water wanders down rocks, spreads and slows
to a pattern that holds, builds, becomes below
dry stream and limestone caves: the echoed call

that reaches us as we strike camp unaware.
Breaks in the cliff face trace like tears
in living skin. We are anticipated everywhere. . .
at the heart of the canyon, along rockfall.

Grand Canyon
Amil Quayle

I speak now of that Grand Canyon
which lies within each of us. There
are pre-Cambrian rocks at the center,
the core, and talus from yesterday's fall;
marble and granite grown hard from the
pressure and heat of heartbreak and
passion; crumbling sandstone, layer on
layer of sediment, sentiment piled on
over a lifetime's experience. The sun
bursts on us each morning then dies
and we are in darkness, but moon shadows
tease our walls. We listen to the pulsating
rhythm of time's river lapping at our
shores. The sandy places slide, diffuse,
move closer to the sea. A billion years
of erosion is magnified, demagnified into
sixty or seventy years as we measure time.
Perhaps in a million years your shinbone
will be a fossil in another Grand Canyon,
cold in a bed of rock next to mine.

Making All Things New
Parker J. Palmer

They say the layered earth rose up
ancient rock leviathan
trailing ages in its wake
lifting earthmass toward the sun
and coursing water cut the rock away
to leave these many-storied walls
exposé of ages gone
around this breathless emptiness
more wondrous far
than earth had ever known

My life has risen layered too
each day each year in turn has left
its fossil life and sediments
evidence of lived and unlived hours
the tedium the anguish yes the joy
that some heart-deep vitality
keeps pressing upward
toward the day I die

And Spirit cuts like water though it all
carving out this emptiness
so inner eye can see
the soaring height of canyon walls within
walls whose very color, texture, form
redeem in beauty all my life has been
the darkness and the light, the false, the true
while deep below the living waters run
cutting deeper through my parts
to resurrect my grave-bound heart
making, always making, all things new.

In the River
Philip Wofford

In the river,
 in the fluid,
  in the wetness
of my own blood,
 I know my body
  is a beautiful canyon
 slowly being worn down
 to nothing.
And beyond my personal continent,
 other bodies
  and river lives
   work with and against
  each other,
   seeking some final balance
   between the search
   for an ocean to easily and
    without thought
     flow into
   and a time allotted for this search
 in which MANBODY, VILLAGEBODY,
   NATIONBODY, WORLDBODY,
    are worn, torn
     and wasted away
    without getting anywhere.
 And body means
 the soul that lives there
 housed and deserting its house
 the body,
 by hookcrook
 and random forgetfulness
  of how far it can fly
   without losing sight of
    known topography—
   that place where a single life
   in a time alone
   at a certain moment
   starts to carve its way

starting
to be
to find a way to join
to make
a canyon
to the ocean.

The solace of geology
Lee Patton

arises from everything getting pulverized."
Eventually, he meant, in geologic ages'
patience and the fury of tectonic rages.

"Everything?" I challenged. The geologist
and I stared upwards, sharing my whiskey,
seated on his log. Sheer slabs, multi-

colored in weddingcake layers of granite,
sandstone, and shale—each an epoch of
metamorphosis, erosion and grit sloughed,

buried, rising again to be sunk again
in flood and drought and lava catastrophe—
climbed in our sights from redbud canopy

clear up to canyon rim. "Everything? Won't
humans' layer consist of polyester, chrome,
diapers, lard, petrified sewage foam—

won't our short human episode be a stain
of garbage between great layers of schist
and gneiss?" "But nothing human'll persist,"

the geologist insisted. "You must accept
the grinding power of sheer tonnage and time
versus the gunky waste and tuneless rhymes

of humankind, our flicker of futile acts
in the vastness of a volcanic, fiery planet's
endless energy and urges. Geology's a bandit

who commutes its loot back to raw material."
Maybe I confused whiskey haze with blind hope,
but his words soothed. Was I a misanthrope?

"Everything? Meaning all orange traffic cones,
all junk mail carried Deliverable to Addressee
Only to my door as a burden for my elderly,

limping postman? People who say 'orientate'?
Cadillac off-road SUVs? Escalators that force
us to wander in merchandise without recourse,

lost in some third-floor hell of undergarments
and wedding registries with no route back down?
The undeserving rich? Scary burger clowns?

The bones of officials who send young citizens
off to die in distant wars?" "Yes, their bones,"
the geologist affirmed. "And mine. And yours."

In Blacktail Canyon
Bill Noble

You're always upstream of Crystal Rapids,
the boatmen say, wry and open-faced,
speaking of fate. But not here, not now.

A wave—bigger than any animate thing
you had ever encountered—licked you
from your boat, swallowed you. Down its icy throat
into its belly, into no-breath, into whirl.

Then quick hands grasped your vest
and you were vaulted up and into life again,
to sprawl face to face, body pressed to living body,
wordless, in the bottom of the spinning boat.

And now you come alone up Blacktail Canyon,
up the shadowed chattering thread of water
deep in the glowing thousand-layered sandstone.
Maidenhair, gossamer and green, drips from every seep,
this fragile fern we name
with such unexpected intimacy.

You sit for unmeasured time
feeling Crystal twine itself
into the brief chemistry of your brain,
into the deep, wavering trace of Blacktail Canyon,
into the rolling Earth.

A linnet's carol, silvered by the canyon,

falling around you,
note by note.

Stillness and motion.
Chance.

You sip sweet limestone water,
then move away,
out of song and silence,
downstream once more,
toward Crystal Rapids.

What You Think About Rafting through
the Grand Canyon on the Eighth Day of Rain
Terry Martin

Call it lightning, call it thunder, call it wind,
the canyon says *You need to know this.*

Teeth chattering, you remember
other canyons, smaller gulches, gorges, gullies.
You think of chasm, fissure, cleft and gap,
how notch and split can lead to opening.

Carrying little, pockets empty, you think about
the world behind and its comforts—
hot water, clean clothes, dry beds—
of mornings slept through, food eaten without tasting,
the sleepwalking trance of inattention
that domesticity allows.

Wet and shivering in your yellow raft,
you know this river's path
is the only one imaginable now.
There is no turning back.

Scuffed and bruised, you think about
flooding arroyos and washes,
torrents of mud, gravel, water roaring,
pouring down red cliffs into the roiling river.
About thunder louder and clouds darker
than you've heard or seen before,
about grey sky and brown water
you know could swallow you.

Approaching Crystal, you tighten your life jacket
and think of trusting guides and what they know,
how they read in water what you can't see.

On the eighth day of rain,
you think about how a storm, too, can be a poem.
And you look forward to day's end, when, cold and tired,
you and your friends will pull to a new shore,
unload gear, set up the kitchen, pitch tents, pour wine.
How you'll shake wet sand from your shoes,
how staccato raindrops will punctuate your tent,
how the next rapid's song will lull you to sleep.

August 16, 1869
Charles Hood

Every day
horizon flat against jaw
                    scrapes Dunn
into raw rind.
A vertical mile of sky
ramrods down his throat
and it would take days to crawl to the rim
to a place where you could even run a quarter mile
in a straight line.

Every day
they crash and swim.
Emma Dean's bow
is a mess. The rations
stink. Rapids cluster
like flies. A beach and logs for oars
and prancing blue tributary
are as welcome as angels,
and so named. Powell studies tiers
of unconformity; the rest sleep
and mend
while he transects the ruins.

"It is ever a source of wonder to us why these ancient people
sought such inaccessible places for their houses."
                    "Doubtless,
some of these people preferred another alternative,
and rather than be baptized or hanged
they chose to imprison themselves
within these canyon walls."

A flight of egrets:
the Bright Angel's
robe.

Bessie's Honeymoon, 1928*
Andrea Ross

> *Oh mama dear please come:*
> *My dolly must be drowned.*
> *When I put her in the creek,*
> *She sank without a sound.*
>   *-from Bessie Hyde's personal journal*

We paused at Lee's Ferry
Jeremiah said to abandon the trip
but we swept our scow, now named
Rain-in-the-Face, away.

The inner gorge shadowed us with after-rain
agave smell. A wild sheep's horn curled
against the canyon's wall,
scree twinkling to the starry-cold river.
Crystal Rapid exploded between boulders,
washing us through the river's middle,
pebbles popping against the floor.
Glen pulled hard on the sweeps while I pushed:
this was more than the marriage-night—
shooting a rapid is an act of love.

Black schist radiated the day's heat into evening,
so we moored above Fern Glen Rapid to curl
to the cool rocking planks and slept in water's din

At Lava Falls
We dropped the ledge
dove into the churning
that splintered our sweeps
tore all gear from the scow
The Colorado sang as it ground us

One bail-bucket has all but its rim ripped off
leaving a shark-jaw shape still clipped to the boat
we sort out wet blankets on the beach
cull dry flour-lumps from slurry
what will it be like to leave?

We'll miss this when we're gone
starts now.

* Bessie and Glen Hyde attempted to run the Colorado River through the
Grand Canyon on their honeymoon in 1928. They were advised against
doing the trip but went anyway and disappeared somewhere below Lava
Falls. Bessie's and Glen's bodies were never found. If they had completed the
trip, Bessie would have been the first woman known to boat the length of
the canyon. There is still speculation as to whether they survived the trip and
escaped the canyon.

Lava Falls
Vaughn Short

Now there rages a rapid wild—
Lava Falls is its name.
One mad ride upon its waves
And you'll never be the same.

Deep they say still water flows,
But it isn't half the fun
As that which boils, heaves, and churns
Down this rock-strewn run.

To Lava came a limp old raft,
Surplus from World War Two.
On a lucky try at water low
It once had made it through.

It paused there upon the brink
With apprehension, fear, and doubt.
Could it survive that awesome plunge?
Last chance to chicken out!

No matter how the water churns,
No matter how wild the ride,
This is no time for turning back—
For there's such a thing as pride.

So down into the surging falls
Eased the ancient boat.
The heaving torrent gathered it in—
Now it's sink or float.

How this old raft will heave and plunge.
Turn, tumble, toss, and spin,
But even if it makes it through
It can really never win.

For if it ever comes once more
To pause there on the brink,
There'll always be that nagging doubt,
It still could flip or sink!

Swimming Grand Canyon
Rebecca Lawton

I.

Georgie wore leopard print
    swimsuits and cyan sunpants
Long ago the wind
leathered her skin

She squinted above my cap
    though the sun was not in her eyes
She claimed she didn't mind
flipping boats on the river

A can of beer in both hands
    clinging at dawn at Lee's Ferry
she said it again:
    Having a boat flip
    in the rapids
      is a way of life for me

She stood with her lead boatman
    smiling, burly, naked
    from the waist up
Behind them, swampers
bent to loading G-rigs
    as crystalline stars
    dimmed overhead

II.

Georgie first swam Grand Canyon
    when it was warmer
    before the dam

She began river life
after the death of her only girl
    keeping at it until
    she passed at eighty-one
She became legend:
    Woman of the River

III.
Having a boat flip
means swimming
brain-chilling water
First your limbs go numb

in current, icy
from black-bottomed Lake Powell
You swim with legs of lead

You may succumb
to the rule of fifty:
> *Fifty-degree water yields*
> *fifty-fifty odds*
> *of surviving fifty minutes*

IV.
Georgie always said
if she could find a man
> who gave her the same thrill
> as the river
she'd marry him

As she spoke, she never looked
straight at me. Her stare
hurled into the distance
Maybe she saw clearly
> what lay ahead
and didn't care

Within two years
she'd lost two more
> one her smiling lead boatman
> one her best friend
> washed out at Lava Falls

Nothing could bring back Rose,
her lost darling
Swimming Grand Canyon
is a way of life for me
and an enjoyable one
at that

Letter to a Young Swamper
Peter Anderson

It is the summer of 1976, you have just turned twenty, and you have landed your dream job. You arrive at Lee's Ferry in a U-Haul truck full of vintage World War II rubber. And as you are blowing shop-vac air into two long outrigger tubes soon to be strapped to an aluminum frame which is itself strapped to an elongated rubber donut that holds this whole scow together, you realize that, yes, this boat is a pig compared to those powered only by muscle and oars, but at least you won't have to run that triple-rig on the beach beside you, where an old and leathery LA woman in a faux leopard-skin bathing suit drinking an early morning Coors orders around her harum of boatmen who are inflating not one, but three big rafts lashed side-by-side. Your boat is a thirty-three foot barge, sleek in comparison, which will ferry you, the head boatman, fifteen passengers, a weeks worth of groceries, cases upon cases of cold beer, and a porta-potty, also known as the groover, down the Colorado to Lake Mead. You will spend ten days riding in the back of the barge, savoring the changing palette of limestones, sandstones, and shales that seduced you after that first trip down the river years ago. And you will breathe in the fumes of a Mercury outboard, admiring the skills of your ex-army boss boatman who pirouettes your barge around massive boils of whitewater foaming up out of huge river craters that could swallow a mobile home without spitting out the evidence. Clearly, the river says, you do not know your ass from a hole in the ground.

Now you have a few trips under your belt and you are a seasoned swamper, which is another way of saying Big Ditch longshoreman (without union pay) who occasionally runs a rapid or two, but who mostly ferries stuff from boat to beach and beach to boat, bushwacks through tamarisk thickets looking for a weedy trunk thick enough for a bow-line tie down, pumps air back into the neoprene pig in the cool canyon morning, and digs the daily pit underneath the groover. This is not glamorous work, but at least you know the difference between your ass and *this* hole in the ground.

Soon you are beginning to dream the river at night. It helps that you sleep out on the boat—your barge is good for that—although you do wake from time to time imagining you have come unmoored and are headed downriver to Crystal. You jump up and check the rope and thank Tao you are still tethered to solid ground, so you climb back into your bag. And before it is time to get up and kindle a fire for morning coffee, you savor a few dreamtime lines—gracefully steering your rig down through the rocky-fanged gap at the head of Horn Creek or gliding down one tongue of glassy green water after another into the shining good time waves of Turquoise, Sapphire, and Ruby. Later during your waking hours, you accept a pinch of Copenhagen from your boot camp boss after Havasu, which helps you stay awake as you motor the long stretch of post-lunch flat water down to Lava Falls, where you go up on the ledge above the river and stare into the great frothing mess of the BIGONE until the columnar lines in the basalt across the river seem to be melting in the sun. Your mind wanders while your boot camp boss describes his line through Lava. And then he says, "Well, are you ready to run it?" And you hope like hell, as you walk back down that rocky trail toward your nervous passengers, that at least for a few choice river moments, you will know your ass from a hole in the ground.

It has been five years or so since you abandoned your motor rig apprenticeship, and you have been rowing smaller boats down mountain rivers. And now the time has come for your first private trip back down through your old swamping grounds. You row a thirteen-foot Miwok down the river you once knew only on the big rigs and you feel incredibly small, but not so small that you don't chase a line between two huge holes, which erupt into a cauldron of foam that sends you ass-over-teakettle faster than you can say Sockdolager, and you are gasping for breath under the bottom of your boat for the first time. But the rest of the trip goes well, and you run into your old outfit at Diamond Creek and there's your boot camp boss loading rubber into a U-Haul and you remember your first run through Lava and how he toasted you out on the barge after dinner that night. On the road out of Diamond Creek, you recall the underwater terror of that run gone wrong in "Sock," but even a bad line will get you further down the river…a little closer, if you're paying attention, to knowing your ass from a hole in the ground.

A few decades later, you will drive your oldest daughter up the old road past Marble Canyon and the turnoff to Lee's Ferry, past Vermilion Cliffs where your boot camp river boss once lived and maybe still does and where there used to be a great little honkytonk for boatmen between trips, where you vaguely recall chasing a girl or two, where you once listened in awe, albeit from a few barstools down—you were only a young punk swamper after all—to your river elders telling tales…how Jimmy Hall hustled some chump using a shovel handle for a pool cue or how that big-hearted soul you knew only as Whale powered through the hole in Crystal. You will think of them as you drive up the switchbacks of the Kaibab, which you once rode down on the roof of the company U-Haul, and then you will forget about them as you follow the dirt road out to the North Rim. And as you look down from Point Sublime, through the Big Empty, toward that thread of a river, which you have not been on for over thirty years, you will wonder, since you're now approaching sixty, if you will ever row your daughters down that river. Sure you will. You must. You have to show them the canyon from the river up, this place where maybe you learned the difference between your ass and a hole in the ground. Where at least you know now, they really aren't that far apart.

Bass Camp, Mile 108
Margaret Randall

Light retreats along the massive wall of rock
pale sculpture of Shinumo Quartzite
and Hakatai Shale
until only its uppermost reaches
pulse in flame.
Burnished ribbon of copper,
sudden spit of gold
racing along their fluted edges.

Massive vertical tipped in purest light,
blinding the senses,
recharging the breath,
running backwards
until it spends itself
in that one last thread
final lick at the edge of time
five thousand feet above.

The dusky face loses its definition then.
Velvet settles into gentle folds.
Shadow descends
accompanied by night's symphony:
cicadas, frogs, the tiny feet of scurrying field mice
and curiosity of ring-tailed cats.

Disappearing light has taken my questions
and coiled them tight
in the hollow of my throat.
I touch its pulse
with the middle fingers of my left hand
and remember who I am.

The River Scrapes against Night
Wendy Mnookin

Through the scrim of the tent
I map constellations.
No matter how hard I stare,
I can't find the boundaries
between river and canyon,
canyon and sky. Bats
swoop close, intimate,
alarming. Night keeps knocking
without a hint of politeness.
I'm not fooled
by steady breathing.
We are this small.
This brief.

EMERGENCE

A Road to the Upper World
Albert Yava, as told to Harold Courlander

The people who wanted to escape from the Third World decided to send a scout up to see what it was like up there and make contact with Masauwu. They chose a swift bird, the swallow. The swallow was swift, all right, but he tired before he reached the sky and had to come back. After that they sent a dove, then a hawk. The hawk found a small opening and went through, but he came back without seeing Masauwu. Finally they sent a catbird. He was the one that found Masauwu.

Masauwu asked him, "Why are you here?"

The catbird said, "The world down below is infested with evil. The people want to come up here to live. They want to build their houses here, and plant their corn."

Masauwu said, "Well, you see how it is in this world. There isn't any light, just greyness. I have to use fire to warm my crops and make them grow. However, I have relatives down in the Third World. I gave them the secret of fire. Let them lead the people up here, and I will give them land and a place to settle. Let them come.

After the catbird returned to the Third World and reported that Masauwu would receive them, the people asked, "Now, how will we ever get up there?" So Spider Old Woman called on the chipmunk to plant a sunflower seed. It began to grow. It went up and almost reached the sky, but the weight of the blossom made the stem bend over. Spider Old Woman then asked the chipmunk to plant a spruce tree, but when the spruce finished growing it wasn't tall enough. The chipmunk planted a pine, but the pine also was too short. The fourth thing the chipmunk planted was a bamboo. It grew up and up. It pierced the sky. Spider Old Woman said, "My children, now we have a road to the upper world. When we reach there your lives will be different. Up there you will be able to distinguish evil from good. Anything that is bad must be left behind down here. All evil medicine must be thrown away before you go up. Sorcerers cannot come with us, or they will contaminate the Fourth World. So be careful. If you see an evil person going up, turn him back."

The people began climbing up inside the bamboo stalk. How they got through the bamboo joints I don't know, because the story doesn't explain about that. The mockingbird guarded them on the way up. He was like a scout. He went ahead, calling, "Pashumayani! Pashumayani! Pash! Pash! Pash!–Be careful! Be careful!" The people came up in groups, until everyone reached the top. The opening in the place where they came out was called the sipapuni. The people camped near where they emerged. The light was grey and they didn't know where they would be going.

Rim
Laurelyn Whitt

Are there horizons
where there is no horizontal

where mountains fold space,
hold distance up?

Embedded in a canyon
our heads tilt instinctively.

Here earth meets sky,
we can reach it; the rim

does not shimmer and recede.

We lean into diagonal lives,
relieved of right angles

eyes, arms, hearts drawn
upward, vectored to ridgelines

keenly aware of the slant
of time, its shape and substance;

it is a wedge; it moves
along ray-stroked slopes;

we pass into it,
are passed over.

Nightwalk, Canyon
Rick Kempa

A drift of skunk. I open my eyes,
blink, and watch the stars one by one
perch on the black ridgeline, then
leap bravely into the brimming sky.

Knowing that day dawns up there hours
before it happens here, I rise, break-
fast, gather my things into my pack,
lace my boots, take my water bottles

to the creek, and grudgingly
set out, following the cone of light
from my headlamp into the still night.
The trail at least is wide, bounded by

the grey mass of cliffs on my left
and, on my right, by a steep plunge
to where the river hisses and churns
through its gorge. Once, I stop, turn off

my lamp. The dark body of the river
swallows the stars, gives nothing back.
A meteor carves its sizzling track—
so lurid, so slow, that I sniff the air

for sulfur. On the rim, a lone light
shimmers: *Attain me. Move.* A cloud
of moths wreathes my head. Bats bombard
me, swerve away at the last instant,

the white bars on their wings blazing.
Sacred Datura beguile me with their
giant full-moon faces. *Stay*, they say.
I try not to think of what I am leaving

behind: a peace that exists only
in this place where I most belong,
an interval that I wholly owned.
I climb neither slowly nor fast toward

the light and all it signifies, scanning
the sky for the first cast of that other light,
so as to be guided yet again in the art
I never mastered, how to return.

Hiking Out
Bernice Lewis

Close the bunkhouse door
Cross the bridge
Pick a trail

Say goodbye
to the river, the schist, the quiet

Head up the trail
each switchback
a blessing
and a curse

Last one out
wins

North Kaibab Trail
Janet B. Eigner

After the heat and dust
walk upgrade along the cool path
canopied in ancient rock,
the granite laced alive with green.
The Bright Angel, in North Rim flight,
percolates nearby,
crimson Penstemon bugling from its bed.
Cross-path, beside Indian Paintbrush's scarlet chimes,
rock-bound plants drip their jewels.
Fuchsia lipsticks nod off the twining Snapdragon.
Pink Beavertail and lemon Prickly Pear,
worn like staircase carpet,.
tesselate the steep cliffs.
Magenta cactus blossoms stir longing,
as you kneel to touch their waxed glory.
Dusk webs us over.
In the willow thicket
deer shades browse the shallows.

Coming Back Out
Judith McDaniel

We sit under that ledge for a day
and a night and when the black drizzle

grays, we pack up and start
the climb out. My friend says

the key is our pace and she leads us
slowly, our footsteps steady as

heartbeats. Packs weighing
like the world above us press down

on our backs. I try not to look up
not to imagine the nine miles ahead

our destination hidden in the mist
and clouds above. For the first hour

I am sure the climb out is not
possible. My feet are bruised and raw

and the pack straps cut my shoulders
with the weight of seven days uneaten food,

a sleeping bag sodden with rain.
One foot, then the other. Eyes cast down,

I watch the pattern of rock beneath,
wonder at the glow of cactus flowers

in the icy sleet, the gray light.
Suddenly we turn around a rock ledge

and find three boys huddled under one
rain poncho. I want to walk on,

keep my focus on putting one foot ahead
of the other, but we stop, ask what's wrong?

Oh, he's tired, says he can't make it,
so we're going to leave him here and go
get our leader to come back for him.
And my pack strap broke so I'm gonna leave
my pack here too. We'll be back,
one assures us, then they head off. The boy
under the poncho shivers, smiles with some
embarrassment at his own weakness. I look
more closely and see the blue shadow
under the line of his lips, the tremor
shaking out from his body core. *Where*
is the leader who is coming back for you?
I want to know. *Up there.* He nods toward
the rim and wraps his arms around his chest
to hold the shaking. *The guys said they'd*
send a ranger in a helicopter for me,
that's what they do when people get stuck.

I have had the same fantasy this morning
so I try to be gentle as I tell him
to look at the fog swirling down, rolling
along the grass, wrapping itself around rock
faces and smothering the light. *My dad's*
the leader, he assures me, *he'll make*
the rangers come and get me. I am
angry now, angry at the interruption of my
meditation, the quiet repetition of step
upon step that was making the climb out
seem possible, angry at a leader who would
leave any child shivering in a wet t-shirt,
angry at this child who believes the impossible.
You're going to walk with us, we tell him
and pull out sweaters, dry socks, a candy
bar, and canteens of gatorade. He stumbles
for a while, but gradually he recovers,
fed, warmed, accompanied, and bounds ahead
on the path, chattering, while I still plod,
placing one foot heavily in front of the other.

Time Line
David Ray

Little more than the width of a hair,
a feather or poem on thin paper—

enough room for my life and yours—
and we are climbing, lifted

by six million years of stone laid down,
our ancestors firmly in place

but alive as isotopes, molecules dancing,
darting, spinning, ever alive,

uncrushably, eternally alive,
and we too are almost glowing.

Origin in Depth
John Nizalowski

My daughters stand at
Yavapai Point, seeing the
canyon for their first time.

It has recently snowed, and
clouds play among the cliffs.
Shadows ripple beneath the
quarter moon and a white sun
teases out brief rainbows over
the red-umber Tower of Ra.

I have told the girls the myth
of the Hopi Emergence, and
they speak to each other of
lines of Indians ascending
from those unsolved depths.

But I imagine instead my
mother, old woman of
Belarusian stock, who
once gazed out from
where her granddaughters
now stand, not long before
she died, wanting to see the
Grand Canyon before leaving
this world for the next sphere.

In her is my origin in deep
time—a small village on the
Lesna River, making its way
to the Baltic Sea, from where
her father migrated west, so
that his great-granddaughters
could stand and see the place
where the Hopi arose to hail
Másaw and their new world.

The Grand Cañon
Mary Austin

Now I know what becomes
Of the many-colored days,
Rose yellow evenings,
Red mornings and the hours
When all the hills
Are low and round like grapes
Amber and purple-juiced,
And the leaf-colored earth
Pulses with light like sap.
Now I know where they go,
Touching Sandia, Jemez, and San Francisco peaks,
Wing and wing to the west.
They are on their way to the Grand Cañon.
There they lie, overlapping
In motionless unreality.
And all the dim blue dawns,
The lost twilights, hyacinth-hued,
Cuddle down in the cleft,
Old as the world
And all its many-colored days.

Bright Angel Point at Sunset
David Lee

> *Thus the light rains, then pours,*
> *The liquid and rushing crystal*
> *beneath the knees of the gods.*
> *-Pound, Canto IV*

The canyon bleeds, then deepens
and darkens. The intricate declension
of its ledges, bluffs and grottos
blends in this late light.
Wind swirls from the depths
carrying pine scent on its back.
A sliver of white moon
in the west. A nighthawk roars above.
Thin light spills into the gorge
and the river sings an ancient song.
At the edge of shadow, night:
dark stone, pine scent, water, cascading light.

Authors' Notes

Co-editor **Peter Anderson** is a former river guide, wilderness ranger, and magazine editor. His books include *First Church of the Higher Elevations*, a book of mountain essays, and *Tracing Time in Stone: A Grand Canyon Journey*, a children's book on geology. He lives on the western edge of the Sangre de Cristo Range in Colorado.

Mary Hunter Austin (1868-1934) was one of the early nature writers of the American Southwest. Her classic *The Land of Little Rain* describes the fauna, flora and people—and evokes the spirituality—of the region between the High Sierra and the Mojave Desert of southern California. Later she moved east to New Mexico and continued to write about the places she loved, including the Grand Canyon.

Joan Baranow writes: "In March 1981 a friend and I took a bus from Tucson to the Grand Canyon on a lark. We spent the first night on the rim, freezing in our flimsy sleeping bags. But the next day we got the last camping spot left and hiked into the canyon. It was a glorious experience!"

S. Omar Barker (1894-1985), an oft-recited cowboy poet, spent most of his life living in the same cabin in New Mexico where he grew up, working as a rancher, teacher and writer. His books include *Vientos de las Sierras* (1924), *Buckaroo Ballads* (1928), and *Rawhide Rhymes: Singing Poems of the Old West* (Doubleday, 1968).

John Barton's eleven books of poetry and six chapbooks include *For the Boy with the Eyes of the Virgin: Selected Poems* (2012), *Balletomane* (2012) and *Polari* (2014). Co-editor of *Seminal: The Anthology of Canada's Gay-Male Poets* (2007), he lives in Victoria, B.C., where he edits *The Malahat Review*.

William Wallace Bass (1849-1933) became one of the first white settlers on the South Rim when he located a camp there in 1884. He was a self-taught geologist and prospector who also wrote poetry, though he was too modest to call it that, referring to his verse as "rhymes and jingles" instead. In fact, he published some of them under that very title, and later, another book entitled, *Adventures in the Canyons of the Colorado.*

Mary Beath's books are *Refuge of Whirling Light*, poems, and *Hiking Alone: Trails Out, Trails Home*, personal essays, both from UNM Press. For five years, she was the designer for Grand Canyon National Park Foundation. She lives in Albuquerque and recently completed a novel that involves uranium mining, *Paradox Valley*.

Bruce Berger is the author of eleven books of nonfiction and poetry. Many of them, including *The Telling Distance*, winner of the Western States Book Award, concern the interactions of nature and culture in desert environments. He was privileged to know Glen Canyon before it was dammed.

Heidi Elizabeth Blankenship spends a great deal of time wandering around the Colorado Plateau, working as a ranger and writing poetry. She is currently stationed on the North Rim of the Grand Canyon.

Chana Bloch's *Swimming in the Rain: New and Selected Poems* was published by Autumn House in 2015. Bloch is co-translator of the "Song of Songs," Yehuda Amichai's *Selected Poetry* and his *Open Closed Open*, and *Hovering at a Low Altitude: The Collected Poetry of Dahlia Ravikovitch*. (www.chanabloch.com)

Michael Blumenthal's collection of short stories, *The Greatest Jewish-American Lover in Hungarian History*, was published by Etruscan Press, who also published his eighth book of poems, *No Hurry: Poems 2000-2012*. His 1988 trip through the canyon with Grand Canyon Dories was one of the highlights of his adult life.

An East Lansing, Michigan poet, **Dorothy Brooks** earlier taught on the Navajo Reservation in Shiprock, NM, for seven years. Excerpts from her memoir about that experience appeared in *Weber—the Contemporary West* in Spring 2013. Her chapbook of poems, *Swamp Baby*, (Finishing Line Press) came out in 2012.

Fred Dings is author of two books of poetry, *Eulogy for a Private Man* (TriQuarterly Books) and *After the Solstice* (Orchises Press). His work has appeared in numerous periodicals, including *The New Republic, The New Yorker, Paris Review, POETRY,* and *TriQuarterly*. He teaches in the MFA program at the University of South Carolina.

Maynard Dixon (1875-1946) spent most of his life in the Southwest. His landscape paintings and murals established him as one of the pre-eminent artists of the early 20th Century American West. He also expressed his love of the West in writing. His collected poems were published by the California Historical Society in 1947.

Janet Eigner documents 12 backpack trips into the Grand Canyon. Her poems appear widely in journals, and on the Poetry Foundation's "American Life in Poetry." Her first full-length poetry book, *What Lasts is the Breath* (Black Swan 2013) was awarded a New Mexico/Arizona Book Award in 2013. (www.eignerdanceswithwords.com)

Ryn Gargulinski is a writer, artist and performer whose poetry, artwork and creative nonfiction is widely published. She reported on many deaths in the Grand Canyon while on staff at an Arizona newspaper, and it's in her nature to turn things into poetry—especially things involving death. More at www.ryngargulinski.com

Thea Gavin, a native of Orange, CA, spent three weeks as National Park Service Artist-in-Residence at the North Rim in June 2011; since then she has returned to the Grand Canyon as often as possible to wander and write.

James Hart retired in 2014 after teaching high school English for 38 years in Brookfield, Missouri, where he lives. His poem, he says, aims "to capture the challenge and futility of putting nature into words as well as to acknowledge the viewer's reverence for the Earth's most ancient places of wonder."

Carol Henrie is a California poet who gardens, dances and writes by moonlight to invite the unexpected. Her poetry was twice recognized with fellowships from the National Endowment for the Arts. Carol's grandparents took their "honey-trip" to the newly designated Grand Canyon National Park in October 1919.

Quaker poet **Phyllis Hoge Thompson**, formerly publishing as Phyllis Thompson, taught poetry in Hawai'i before retiring to Albuquerque. A frequent visitor at the canyon, she and another foolhardy woman, carrying chocolate, an orange, and water, once walked all the way down to the river and back in a single unforgettable day.

Minnesota-born **Bill Holm** (1943-2009) was a poet, essayist, and musician, and the author of twelve books. A graduate of Gustavus Adolphus College in St. Peter, Minnesota and later the University of Kansas, he was Professor Emeritus of English at Southwest Minnesota State University, until his retirement in 2007.

Charles Hood is a Research Fellow at the Center for Art + Environment, Reno. His book *South x South* won the Hollis Summers Poetry Prize. Hood says, "For a while I was homeless and living out of my truck. I spent a lot of time in the Grand Canyon, not all of it in Park Service-approved ways."

Diana Hume George is Professor of English Emerita at Penn State University, Behrend College, and a core faculty member at Goucher College's MFA program in Narrative Nonfiction. She has published ten books of poetry, narrative nonfiction, and literary criticism, and directed writing programs at Penn State and Chautauqua Institution.

Mark Irwin's eighth collection of poetry, *American Urn: New and Selected Poems (1987-2014)*, will be published in 2015. Recognition for his work includes The Nation/Discovery Award, two Colorado Book Awards, four Pushcart Prizes, and fellowships from the Fulbright, Lilly, NEA, and Wurlitzer Foundations.

Hopi artist **Michael Kabotie** (1942-2009) was a founding member of Artist Hopid, a group of five painters who experimented in new interpretations of traditional Hopi art forms and worked together for five years. His book of poetry, *Migration Tears: Poems about Transitions*, was published in 1987 by UCLA.

Carol Kanter's work has appeared in numerous literary journals and anthologies. Finishing Line Press published her two chapbooks, *Out of Southern Africa* (2005) and *Chronicle of Dog* (2006). *No Secret Where Elephants Walk* and *Where the Sacred Dwells, Namaste* (Dual Arts Press, 2010; 2012) marry Carol's poetry to her husband's photography.

Co-editor **Rick Kempa** has been hiking in and writing about the Grand Canyon since 1974. He is also editor of the anthology *ON FOOT: Grand Canyon Backpacking Stories* (Vishnu Temple Press, 2014) and has authored two books of poems, *Keeping the Quiet* and *Ten Thousand Voices*. (www.rickkempa.com)

Ken Lauter has published twelve books of poetry, written several plays, taught at four universities, and worked as a mayor's aide, a university administrator, and an environmental activist. "I lived in Arizona in the 1960s and 1980s, went to the canyon often, and always found it spiritually rejuvenating." (KenLauter.com.)

Rebecca Lawton was among the first women raft guides in Grand Canyon, working a decade on the Colorado between Lee's Ferry and Diamond Creek. Her books include the bestselling *Reading Water: Lessons from the River*, the river novel *Junction, Utah*, and *Steelies and Other Endangered Species: Stories on Water*. (www.beccalawton.com)

David Lee lived in Southern Utah and taught at Southern Utah University for 32 years. A perpetual hiker and quasi-nomad, he was a frequent canyon visitor. Retired, he splits his time between Bandera, Tejas and Seaside, Oregon, where he continues working toward his goal of becoming a World Class Piddler.

Stephen Lefebure has spent much of his life in New Mexico and Colorado exploring the Four Corners States. He has visited the confluence of Bright Angel Creek and the Colorado River fourteen times.

Bernice Lewis served as Grand Canyon Artist in Residence in 2009. In addition to performing, she teaches songwriting at Williams College and Colorado College. *Dreaming on Location*, her first book of poetry, was released in 2009 and is available at www.bernicelewis.com, along with her CD's. Her religion is the Grand Canyon.

Rita Maria Magdaleno is a native Arizonan and recreational river-runner. She lives in Tucson and teaches memoir writing. Her poetic memoir, *Marlene Dietrich, Rita Hayworth, & My Mother* was published by University of Arizona Press. Rita has been a writing fellow at Ucross Foundation and Millay Colony for the Arts.

Terry Martin has written and published three books and hundreds of poems, essays, and articles. She has also edited journals and anthologies. Her 19-day raft trip through the canyon in September 2011 with 14 friends was one of the peak experiences of her life. She thinks Vishnu Schist is sexy.

Judith McDaniel, PhD, JD, has lived and hiked in Arizona for 25 years. Since that first descent to the Colorado River, she has returned numerous times—each a different adventure and challenge. Judith teaches literature and writing in the Master of Arts program at Union Institute and University.

Wendy Mnookin's most recent book is *The Moon Makes Its Own Plea* (BOA Editions.) She teaches poetry at Emerson College and at Grub Street, a non-profit writing program in Boston. She wrote this poem after a rafting trip in the Grand Canyon, during which she was alternately ecstatic and terrified. (wendymnookin.com)

Thorpe Moeckel rowed a baggage boat on a canyon trip for Outdoors Unlimited in 1991. Since then, he's explored a lot of watersheds. He lives now near the Upper James River in Western Virginia, where he teaches at Hollins University. He's the author of three books of poetry.

Seth Muller moved from the East Coast to northern Arizona in 2001 for a life of canyon and high-desert adventure. Among his works, he has written *Canyon Crossing: Stories about Grand Canyon from Rim to Rim* and *Heart in the Bony Middle: Poetic Dispatches from Grand Canyon and Plateau Country*.

John Nizalowski left his upstate New York home and moved to the Southwest in the mid-80's, where he became obsessed with exploring canyons. The author of three books—*Hooking the Sun*, *The Last Matinée*, and *Land of Cinnamon Sun*—Nizalowski currently teaches writing at Colorado Mesa University in Grand Junction.

Bill Noble is a California naturalist, poet, and writer, winner of the 1999 Looking Glass Prize. He's run the Grand once, and has spent a cumulative three months below rim, often off-trail. "Blacktail Canyon" is for Michael and Carolyn Ellis and their boatless encounter with Crystal Rapid's rock garden.

Parker J. Palmer founded the Center for Courage & Renewal and has written nine books that have sold over a million copies. He holds a Ph.D. from Berkeley and has been recognized with twelve honorary doctorates. He's made the ten-day trip down the Grand Canyon three times, always with amazement.

A native of California's Mendocino Coast, **Lee Patton** has enjoyed life in Colorado since college. A volunteer for environmental restoration, he worked on invasive plant eradication around Lee's Ferry and survived two river journeys through Grand Canyon. His newest novel, *Fresh Grave in Grand Canyon*, is forthcoming. More at leepatton.net.

Beth Paulson taught English for over twenty years at California State University Los Angeles. Her poems have received three Pushcart Prize nominations. Her new collection is also titled *Canyon Notes* (Mt. Sneffels Press, 2012). Beth has hiked the Grand Canyon, but this poem came after rafting the river with friends in 2009.

Amil Quayle, poet, painter, and river guide, received his PhD from the University of Nebraska in Lincoln. He has taught at UNL, Utah State University, and Idaho State University. His publications include *Pebble Creek* (Slow Tempo Press, 1993), *Grand Canyon and Other Selected Poems* (Black Star Press, 2009), and *Upset in Upset* (Henry's Fork Books, 2005).

Margaret Randall is a poet, essayist, photographer, and social activist living in Albuquerque, New Mexico. She has visited, hiked, and run the Colorado River through Grand Canyon since childhood. Among Randall's recent books are: *The Rhizome as a Field of Broken Bones* (poetry) and *Che On My Mind* (a poet's memoir of Che Guevara).

David Ray's books of poems include *Hemingway: A Desperate Life, After Tagore, When, The Death of Sardanapalus: Poems of the Iraq Wars,* and *Music of Time: Selected & New Poems. The Endless Search* is a memoir. David lives in Tucson, where he continues to write poetry, fiction, and essays. (www.davidraypoet.com)

Danny Rosen lives five miles north of the river, on Colorado's western slope, in the Grand Valley—an upriver portion of the greater canyon system. He pisses in the river every morning (unnamed tributary, Big Salt Wash.) A chapbook, *Ghost of Giant Kudu*, was published in Spring 2013 by Kattywompus Press.

Andrea Ross has worked as an interpretive ranger at Grand Canyon National Park, a wilderness instructor at the United World College of the American West, and a naturalist guide at several environmental education centers. She lives in Philadelphia with her husband and son, and is an English professor at the Community College of Philadelphia.

Along with hiking Grand Canyon trails since she was 15, Arizona native **Jean Rukkila** lived on the South Rim for four summers as the Grandview Fire Lookout. She also rafted the Colorado River as an aide on trips for adults with disabilities.

Once described by H.L.Mencken as "an American in every pulse beat," **Carl Sandburg** (1878-1967) won three Pulitzer Prizes, two for his poetry and another for a biography of Abraham Lincoln. "There goes God with an army of banners," he remarked, upon seeing his first sunset on the rim of the Grand Canyon.

Reg Saner is a longtime Coloradan whose work has won several national prizes. His poetry and essays have been widely published, and included in some 64 anthologies. His essay "The Ideal Particle and the Great Unconformity," from *The Four-Cornered Falcon*, relates time, hikers, and a grain of sand to the Grand Canyon.

Vaughn Short (1923-2010) lived a long and adventurous life. He was a poet of the Colorado River, troubadour of the desert, and orator of the mountain tops. He grew up on a ranch in Southeastern Arizona and especially loved the Grand Canyon and the red rock country farther north.

Laura Tohe is Diné. Her books include *No Parole Today, Making Friends with Water, Sister Nations* (edited), *Tséyi, Deep in the Rock*, and *Code Talker Stories*. Her commissioned libretto, *Enemy Slayer, A Navajo Oratorio* was performed by The Phoenix Symphony Orchestra. She is Professor of Indigenous Literature at Arizona State University.

First captivated by the Grand Canyon on a river trip in the early 1970's, **Ann Weiler Walka** still explores and writes about the backcountry of the Colorado Plateau, both the tangible terrain and the landscape of the imagination. She loves hearing that her work is read aloud in the outback.

Laurelyn Whitt's poems appear in numerous North American journals, such as *Nimrod International, Malahat Review, Tampa Review, Descant,* and *Rattle.* She is the author of three award-winning poetry collections, including *Interstices* (Logan House Press). Her new book, *Tether*, is forthcoming from Seraphim Editions (Woodstock, Ontario). She lives in Minnedosa, Manitoba.

Daniel Williams is an earth poet with work in a diversity of publications, including one haiku aboard the MAVEN explorer orbiting Mars. His career has led him to Yosemite and the Sierra Nevada, which has been a focus of his writing. "The Grand Canyon," he advises "will embrace your spirit."

Steve Wilson, whose work has appeared in journals nationwide, is the author of four collections of poetry, most recently *The Lost Seventh.* Of the Grand Canyon, his most vivid memory is standing on the South Rim with his two young sons, looking down into the vastness of the abyss.

Philip Wofford was born in Arizona in 1935 and lives in Hoosick Falls, NY. He is best known as a painter of large canvasses in the lyrical abstraction style. He is the author of one book of poems, *Grand Canyon Search Ceremony* (Barlenmir House, 1972).

Albert Yava (1888-1980) was a respected Tewa-Hopi elder whose stories and recollections were recorded in *Big Falling Snow: A Tewa-Hopi Indian's Life and Times and the History and Traditions of His People* (edited by Harold Courlander), which weaves personal recollections with legends, ancient traditions and beliefs, and oral histories of the Hopi. Folklorist and anthropologist **Harold Courlander** (1908-1996) authored over thirty books, including the landmark *People of the Short Blue Corn: Tales and Legends of the Hopi Indians* (1970).

Yevgeny Yevtushenko divides his time between Russia and the United States, where he has been teaching at the University of Tulsa and the City University of New York. Yevtushenko is also a prolific poet who has traveled all over the world, writing verses and poems about the places he has visited.

Acknowledgements

"Letter to a Once-Young Swamper" by **Peter Anderson**. Published with permission from the author.

"The Grand Cañon" (excerpt) from *The Children Sing in the Far West*, by **Mary Austin**, 1926. Copyright renewal ©1956 by Houghton Mifflin. Reprinted with permission from Houghton Mifflin.

"Grand Canyon" from *Living Apart* by **Joan Baranow** (Plainview Press, 1999). Copyright © 1999 by Joan Baranow. Reprinted with permission from the author.

"Grand Canyon Cowboy" from *Rawhide Rhymes: Singing Poems of the Old West* by **S. Omar Barker**. Copyright © 1968. Reprinted with permission from the Omar Barker Estate.

"Sunrise, Grand Canyon" from *Hypotheses* by **John Barton** (House of Anansi, 2001). Copyright © 2001 by John Barton. Reprinted with permission from House of Anansi Press and the author.

"A Winter Day at Grand Canyon" from *The Grand Canyon in Poem and Picture* by **William Wallace Bass**, 1909.

"Grand Canyon/West" from *Refuge of Whirling Light* by **Mary Beath** (University of New Mexico Press, 2005). Copyright © 2005 by Mary Beath. Reprinted with permission from UNM Press and the author.

"The Ballad of the Bright Angel" by **Bruce Berger** from *The Geography of Hope: Poets of Colorado's Western Slope*, edited by David Rothman (Conundrum, 2005). Reprinted with permission from the author.

"Reaching Rider Canyon" by **Bruce Berger**. Published with permission from the author.

"Fence Fault" by **Heidi Elizabeth Blankenship**. Published with permission from the author.

"The Grand Canyon" from *Blood Honey* by **Chana Bloch** (Autumn House, 2009). Copyright © 2009 by Chana Bloch. Reprinted with permission from Autumn House Press and the author.